DO IT NOW!

SCIENCE

WILD EXPERIMENTS & OUTDOOR ADVENTURES

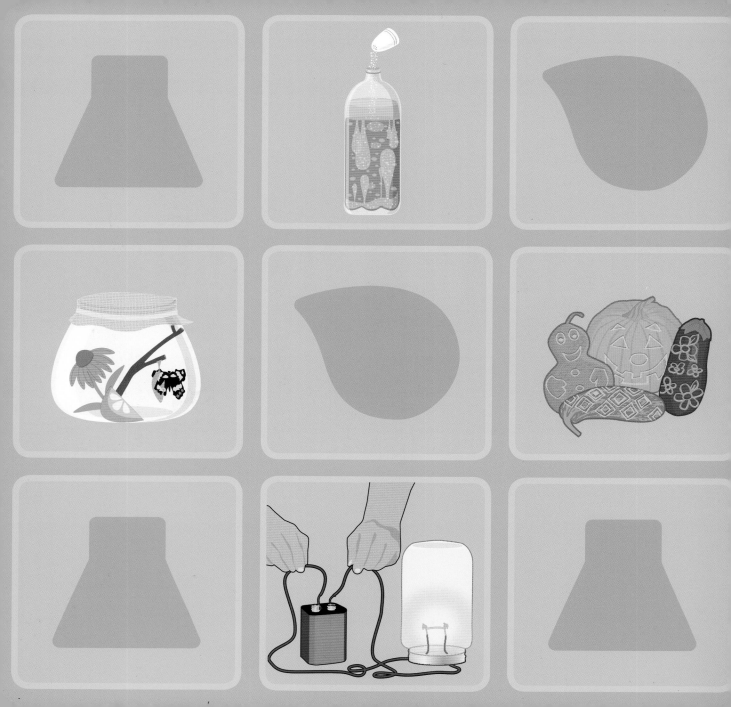

DO IT NOW! SCIENCE

WILD EXPERIMENTS & OUTDOOR ADVENTURES

sarah hines stephens and bethany mann

weldon**owen**

contents

- how to use this book

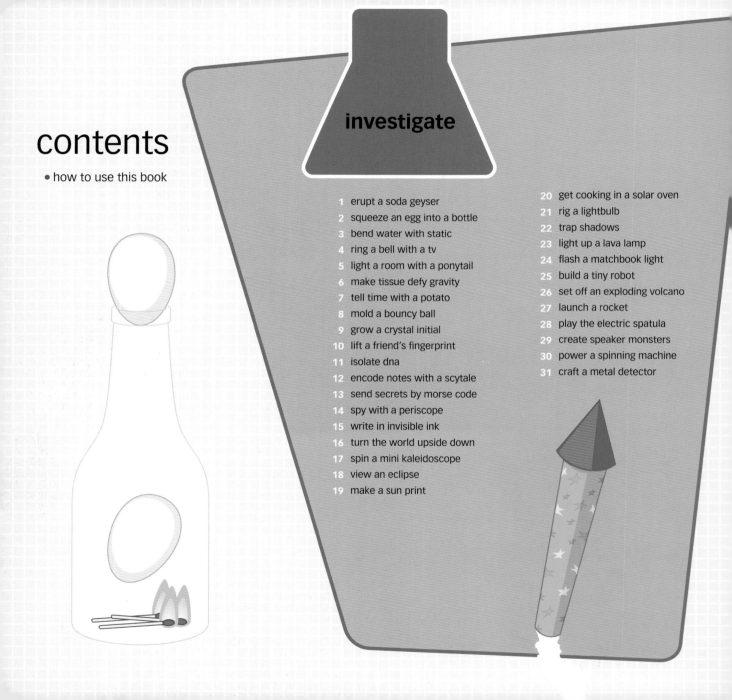

investigate

explore

how to use this book

This is a brand-new type of book—one that uses pictures instead of words to show you how to do all sorts of activities. Sometimes, though, you may need a little extra info. In those cases, look to these symbols to help you out.

TOOLS The toolbar shows the ingredients you'll need to do most projects. Follow the steps to see the amount or measurement that you'll need of each ingredient.

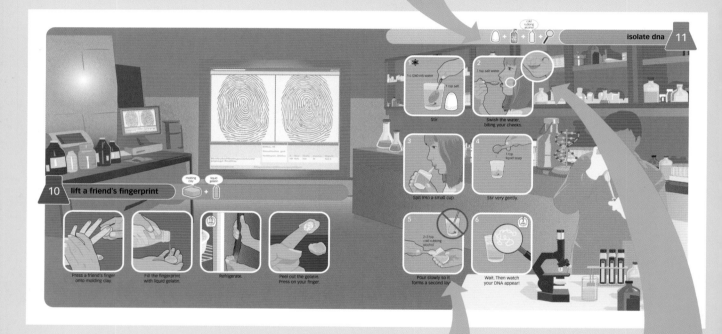

MATH When measurements matter, they'll be written right in the box—like in recipes, or when an item needs to be an exact length. Angle icons show you how far to tilt, and if it's a matter of ratio, icons like 1:1 show you how to get the perfect mix.

3 c
(700 g)   ∠45°   1:1   40 in
(100 cm)

ZOOMS These little circles, placed near or inside a larger frame, draw your attention to bonus information or important details about how to do a step—and sometimes how *not* to do a step.

a word to parents

The activities in this book are designed for children ages ten and older. While we have made every effort to ensure that the information in this book is accurate, reliable, and totally cool, please assess your own child's suitability for a particular activity before allowing him or her to attempt it, and provide adult supervision as appropriate. We disclaim all liability for any unintended, unforeseen, or improper application of the suggestions featured in this book. We will, however, be happy to accept the credit for increased awesomeness.

tool kit

Here are some basic items that you probably have at home, so they aren't listed in the toolbars. Pack a tool kit, and keep it handy!

| scissors | glue | pen, pencil, and marker | plain paper |
| tape | utensils | water | containers |

symbols

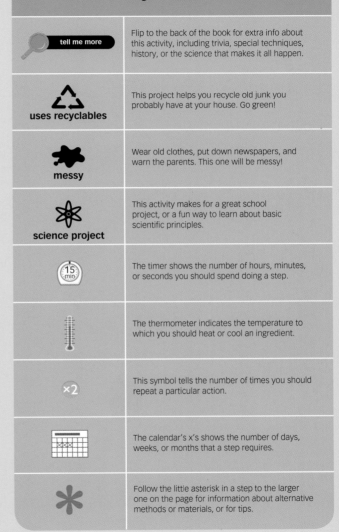

tell me more	Flip to the back of the book for extra info about this activity, including trivia, special techniques, history, or the science that makes it all happen.
uses recyclables	This project helps you recycle old junk you probably have at your house. Go green!
messy	Wear old clothes, put down newspapers, and warn the parents. This one will be messy!
science project	This activity makes for a great school project, or a fun way to learn about basic scientific principles.
(15 min timer)	The timer shows the number of hours, minutes, or seconds you should spend doing a step.
(thermometer)	The thermometer indicates the temperature to which you should heat or cool an ingredient.
×2	This symbol tells the number of times you should repeat a particular action.
(calendar)	The calendar's x's shows the number of days, weeks, or months that a step requires.
*	Follow the little asterisk in a step to the larger one on the page for information about alternative methods or materials, or for tips.

investigate

rotary tool + file + ¾ in (2 cm) pvc pipe + ¾ in (2 cm) pvc endcap + mentos™

4

Tape the pipe to the cap.

5

Drill a hole in the endcap.

6

Drill a hole through the pipe near the tape.

7

Bend the paper clip into a hook. Tie on a long string.

3

Widen the hole so that the candy will fit.

8

Insert the paper clip into the pipe.

2

Drill a hole in the cap.

9

Put the cap on the bottle. Fill with Mentos™.

11 Stand back and yank the string.

10

Add the endcap.

1

Warm the diet cola in the sun. Keep the cap on.

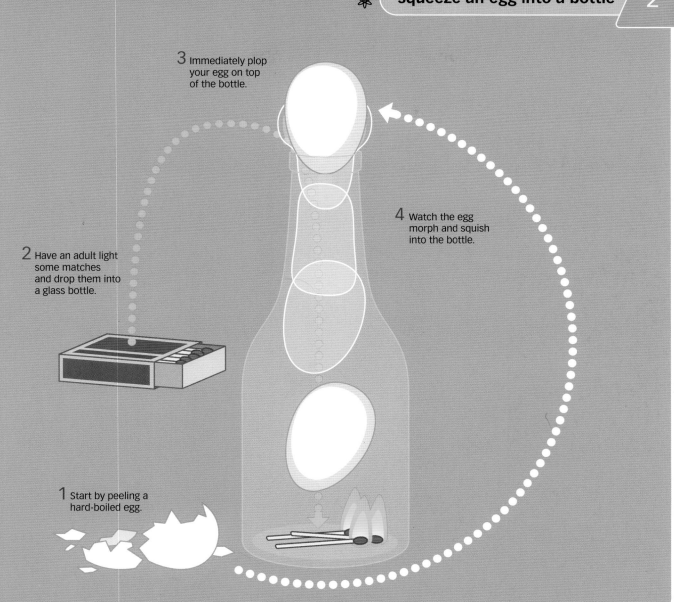

3 Immediately plop your egg on top of the bottle.

4 Watch the egg morph and squish into the bottle.

2 Have an adult light some matches and drop them into a glass bottle.

1 Start by peeling a hard-boiled egg.

bend water with static

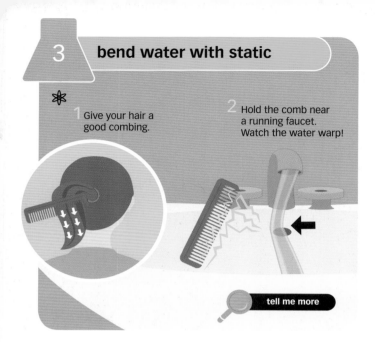

1 Give your hair a good combing.

2 Hold the comb near a running faucet. Watch the water warp!

tell me more

4 ring a bell with a tv

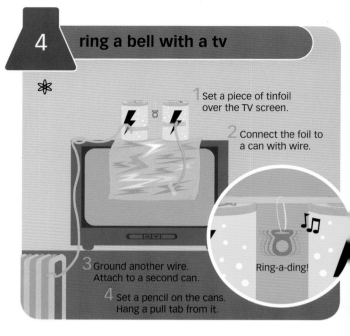

1 Set a piece of tinfoil over the TV screen.

2 Connect the foil to a can with wire.

3 Ground another wire. Attach to a second can.

4 Set a pencil on the cans. Hang a pull tab from it.

Ring-a-ding!

5 light a room with a ponytail

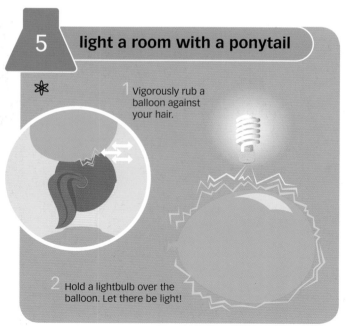

1 Vigorously rub a balloon against your hair.

2 Hold a lightbulb over the balloon. Let there be light!

6 make tissue defy gravity

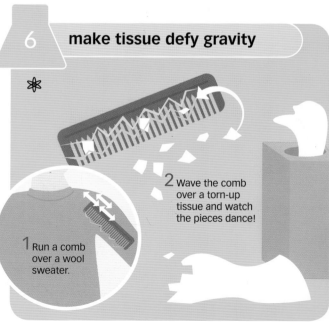

2 Wave the comb over a torn-up tissue and watch the pieces dance!

1 Run a comb over a wool sweater.

galvanized nails + copper wire + + 1200 + wires with alligator clips

tell time with a potato 7

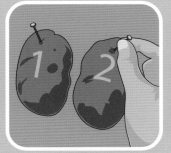
Label your taters.

Press a galvanized nail into each potato.

Stick a copper wire into the other end of each.

Remove the digital clock's battery and battery cover.

Connect potato 1's wire to the positive side.

Link 2's nail to the negative side.

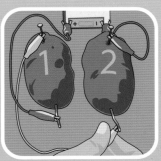
Connect 1's nail to 2's copper wire.

Set your clock to tater-time!

Potatoes aren't the only powerful food in your kitchen—you can make a food clock out of these ingredients, too.

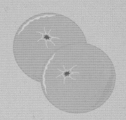

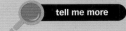
tell me more

 borax cornstarch

½ tsp borax

2 tbsp warm water

Stir to dissolve the borax.

1 tbsp white glue

Pour glue into a jar.

1 tbsp cornstarch

Add cornstarch to the glue.

½ tbsp borax solution

Measure and add the borax solution.

15 sec

Add a few drops of food coloring. Wait.

Stir.

Knead on a clean tabletop.

Roll into a ball.

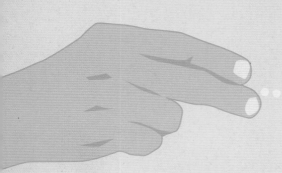

* What *is* this magical borax stuff, anyway? It's a mineral used in makeup and soap. It's also used in bug-killer, so store the ball in a plastic bag when you're done, then wash your hands. Whatever you do, don't eat it!

1. Shape a pipe cleaner. Be sure it will fit into a jar.

2. 3 tbsp borax
1 c (240 ml) very hot water

Carefully add the borax to hot water.

3. 4 drops food coloring

Add coloring. Stir until the borax mostly dissolves.

4. The pipe cleaner should hang above the bottom.

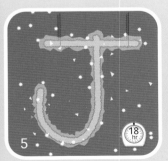

5. 18 hr

Watch your crystals grow.

6. To display, hang your new bling with string.

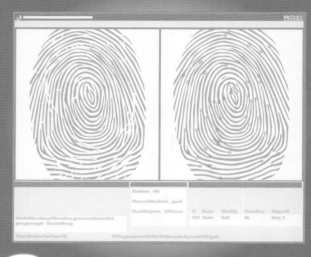

lift a friend's fingerprint

molding clay + liquid gelatin

Press a friend's finger onto molding clay.

Fill the fingerprint with liquid gelatin.

Refrigerate.

Peel out the gelatin. Press on your finger.

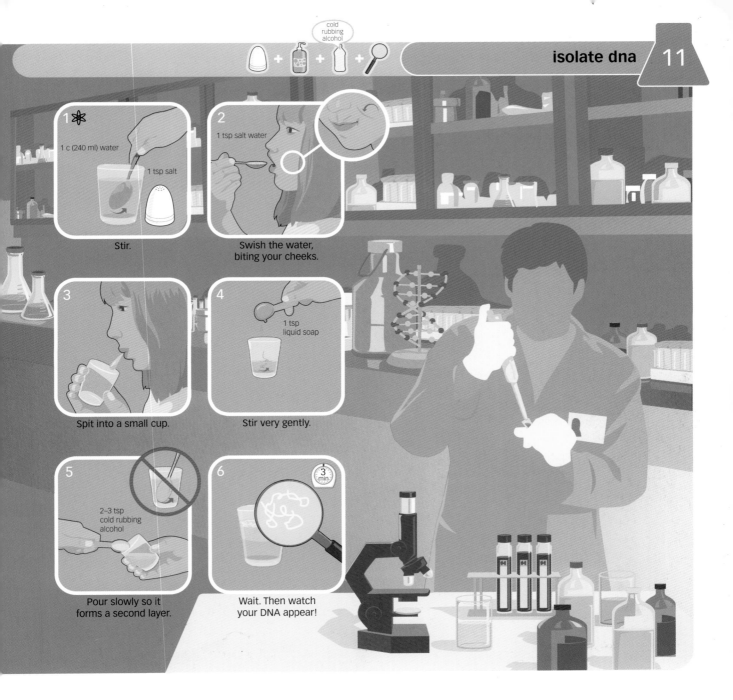

cold rubbing alcohol

1
1 c (240 ml) water
1 tsp salt
Stir.

2
1 tsp salt water
Swish the water, biting your cheeks.

3
Spit into a small cup.

4
1 tsp liquid soap
Stir very gently.

5
2–3 tsp cold rubbing alcohol
Pour slowly so it forms a second layer.

6
3 min.
Wait. Then watch your DNA appear!

encode notes with a scytale

Cut a narrow
paper strip.

Tape and wrap tightly
without overlapping.

Tape the other end.

Write lengthwise, one
letter per blank space.

Unwrap. It's gibberish!
Pass to a trusted pal.

Your friend decodes it
with her own pencil.

Change up the objects you wrap the messages
around to keep your communications extra safe.

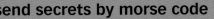
★ = quick flash
— = long flash

a	★ —	n	— ★	1	★ — — — —
b	— ★ ★ ★	o	— — —	2	★ ★ — — —
c	— ★ — ★	p	★ — — ★	3	★ ★ ★ — —
d	— ★ ★	q	— — ★ —	4	★ ★ ★ ★ —
e	★	r	★ — ★	5	★ ★ ★ ★ ★
f	★ ★ — ★	s	★ ★ ★	6	— ★ ★ ★ ★
g	— — ★	t	—	7	— — ★ ★ ★
h	★ ★ ★ ★	u	★ ★ —	8	— — — ★ ★
i	★ ★	v	★ ★ ★ —	9	— — — — ★
j	★ — — —	w	★ — —	0	— — — — —
k	— ★ —	x	— ★ ★ —		
l	★ — ★ ★	y	— ★ — —		
m	— —	z	— — ★ ★		

If you want to send a secret message across the street, all you need is Morse code and a flashlight. Using the guide at left, write out your message letter by letter, then flash it when the time is right.

Your partner will understand you better if you count to three with your light off between each letter and count to seven with the light off between each word.

tell me more

Are there words or phrases you and your friends say a lot? Make up a shortcut instead of spelling it out. Here are some examples.

★ — ★ — ★   "My brother is a dork."
— — ★ — ★   "Gotta go—my mom's coming!"
— — — ★ —   "Whatever!"
— ★ ★ ★ —   "You're my BFF."

spy with a periscope

1
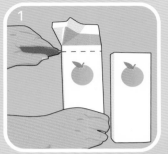
Cut the tops off two cartons.

2

Cut a window near the bottom of one carton.

3
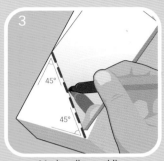
45°
45°
Mark a diagonal line as tall as your mirror.

4

Cut on the line; repeat on the carton's opposite side.

5
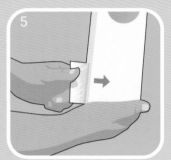
Slide a mirror into the slot. Secure with tape.

6

Look in the window—you should see the ceiling.

7

Repeat the process on the second carton.

8
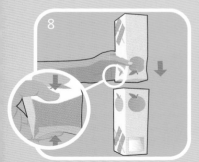
Flip one. Insert with the window facing backward.

9
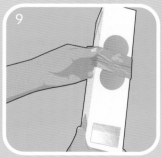
Tape securely.

10

Decorate your periscope.

11

Get your spy on!

Juice half a lemon.

Paint a message with the juice. Let it dry.

Hand the "blank" paper to a friend.

Heat reveals your juicy secret!

 If you want to get extra stealthy, wait for the lemon juice to dry, then write a decoy message in regular ink on top. When you heat the paper, the secret message will rise to the top!

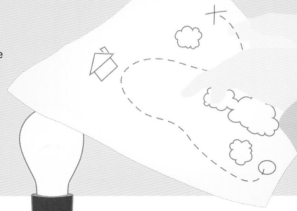

turn the world upside down

Make this simple device and point it at a window. You'll see a topsy-turvy projection.

1 Poke a hole in a plastic cup.

2 Trim wax paper to fit over the cup.

3 Secure it with a rubber band.

4 Turn out the lights and hide under a blanket to see the world flip out!

tell me more

empty pill bottle + clear plastic lid + old CD + super glue

Saw off a bottle's bottom and its cap's top.

Trace the cap onto a lid three times and cut.

Glue circles to the cap top and the bottle top.

Make a stencil the same length as the bottle. Cut out.

Trace onto the CD. Cut out.

Slide in the CD strips. Trim to fit.

Glue a window to the bottom of the bottle.

Draw a pattern on the cap window.

Decorate the bottle. Put beads in the cap and screw on.

Be careful! If you look straight at an eclipse, you'll injure your eyes. Instead, use a handy eclipse viewer for your own private sun show!

1

Tape a sheet of paper inside a box.

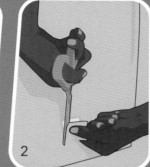

2

Cut an opening opposite the paper.

3

Tape tinfoil over the opening. Prick a hole.

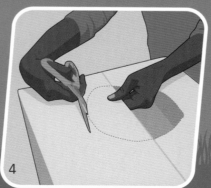

4

Cut a space for your head.

Use the longest box you can find to get an extra-large projection.

 +  +  + +

Gather some
interesting objects.

Arrange the pieces
on cyanotype paper.

Set a clear cover on
top. Leave in the sun.

Remove everything.

Rinse the paper in
a pan of water.

Set on paper to dry. A
sun print appears!

 tell me more

black construction paper   plastic sheet

Draw a square on a pizza box lid near the edges.

Cut along three of the lines to make a flap.

Open the flap and fold it back.

Wrap and tape tinfoil inside the flap.

insulated copper wire + + + picture-hanging wire   + 6-volt dry cell battery

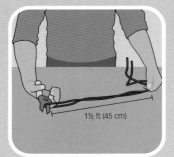

Cut a copper wire in half.

1½ ft (45 cm)

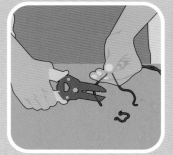

Strip the insulation from the ends.

Poke holes in the lid of a glass jar.

Bend the wires through and shape into hooks.

Line the inside of the box with tinfoil.

Set a piece of heavy black paper on the bottom.

Prop the top open so it gets lots of sunlight.

Add a treat and cover with clear plastic.

✳ Once the light burns out, give the wires plenty of time to cool off before touching!

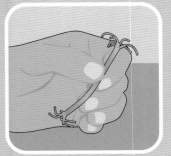

Unravel the ends of a bit of picture wire.

Twist the wire ends around the hooks.

Add the jar.

Touch the wires to the battery terminals.

trap shadows

1 Cover a wall with glow-in-the-dark paint.

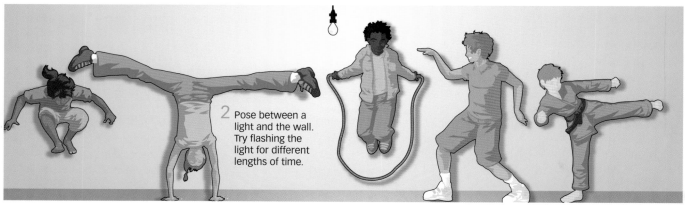

2 Pose between a light and the wall. Try flashing the light for different lengths of time.

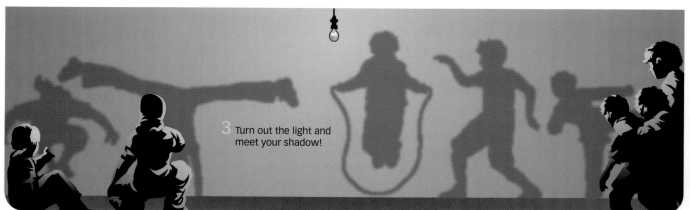

3 Turn out the light and meet your shadow!

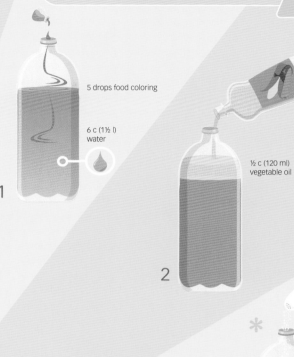

5 drops food coloring

6 c (1½ l) water

1

½ c (120 ml) vegetable oil

2

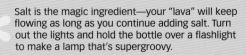

3

*

4

* Salt is the magic ingredient—your "lava" will keep flowing as long as you continue adding salt. Turn out the lights and hold the bottle over a flashlight to make a lamp that's supergroovy.

+   2 LED bulbs + watch battery

Remove the matches.

Mark two dots where
the lights will go.

Poke two holes.

Insert the LED wires.

Tape both left-hand wires
to the matchbook.

Slide the battery under the
loose right-hand wires.

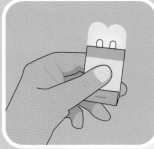

Press to test your light.

Tape the edges of the
battery to the matchbook.

Shine on!

salsa cup + + superglue + double-stick foam tape + vibrating cell-phone motor + + + watch battery

Apply double-stick foam tape to the cup's top.

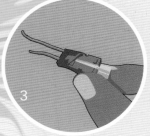

Take the vibrating motor from an old cell phone.

Glue fringe to a clean salsa cup.

Give your 'bot plenty of room to zip around.

Slip the battery between the wires. It's alive!

Attach the motor. Bend one wire up.

Decorate your 'bot.

set off an exploding volcano

vinegar

1 Tape a tin can to a cardboard box top.

2 Wad up newspaper and tape around the can.

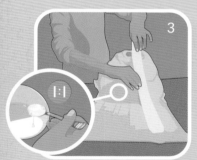

3 Form a volcano with paper dipped in flour and water.

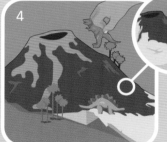

4 Let dry. Decorate with paint and action figures.

5 Fill the can halfway with baking soda.

6 Fill with vinegar dyed with food coloring.

film
canister

toilet
paper

vinegar

launch a rocket 27

Roll an open film canister
or plastic jar in paper.

Tape the tube around
the canister.

Cut out a paper circle and
make a slit to the center.

Fold it into a cone
and tape it on top.

Pour baking soda onto
a square of toilet paper.

Tape it into a packet and
take everything outdoors.

Set the packet in
the canister lid.

Fill half the canister with
vinegar. Put on the lid.

Flip the rocket over and
stand back for blastoff!

You're building a pretty
powerful rocket here.
Always point it away from
people and windows!

play the electric spatula

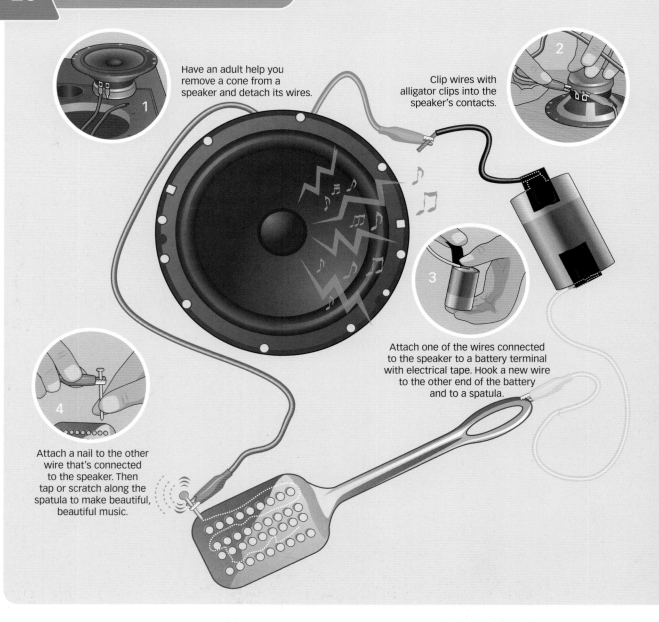

Have an adult help you remove a cone from a speaker and detach its wires.

Clip wires with alligator clips into the speaker's contacts.

Attach one of the wires connected to the speaker to a battery terminal with electrical tape. Hook a new wire to the other end of the battery and to a spatula.

Attach a nail to the other wire that's connected to the speaker. Then tap or scratch along the spatula to make beautiful, beautiful music.

½ c (60 g) cornstarch 1 c (240 ml) water

Mix cornstarch and water together.

Pour onto a baking tray.

Turn a speaker on its side and cover in plastic wrap.

*

Set the pan on the speaker and crank it up.

 What music do speaker monsters like? Turns out they dance better to a specific kind of sound, called a sine wave. Have your parents help you find one on the Internet and play it at about 50 hertz.

nail polish   magnet

Wrap the battery in
electrical wire; trim.

Remove the battery; loop
the wire through the coil.

Strip the plastic coating
off the wire's ends.

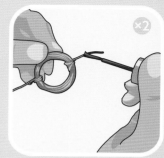

Coat the ends of the wire
in nail polish.

Place the battery on
the magnet.

Add a safety pin
to each end.

Thread the coil's ends
through the pins; tape.

Give it a spin!

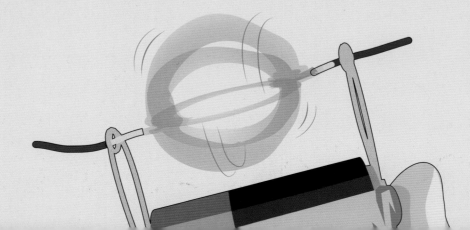

Apply double-stick tape to the backs.

Tape both inside the CD case.

Turn the radio to AM band.

Tune to static at the top of the dial.

Bend the case to hear a tone.

Unbend until the tone stops.

Glue the case to a ruler at that angle.

The tone will resume when you find metal!

explore

set up a solar compass

Place a tall, straight stick in the ground.

Mark the end of the shadow. Wait.

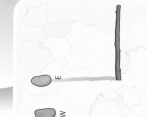

Mark the new end of the shadow.

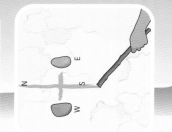

Connect the marks, then make a cross.

This compass is more accurate the closer you are to the equator and the equinoxes. Once you've set it up, you can mark the end of the stick's shadow every hour to make a sundial.

make a magnetic compass

The needle will align along the north-south axis. You'll have to use other clues, like the sun's position in the sky, to tell which end of the needle points north.

Make a windproof puddle.

Rub a needle against a magnet.

Set the needle on a leaf in the puddle.

The needle aligns with the poles.

tell me more

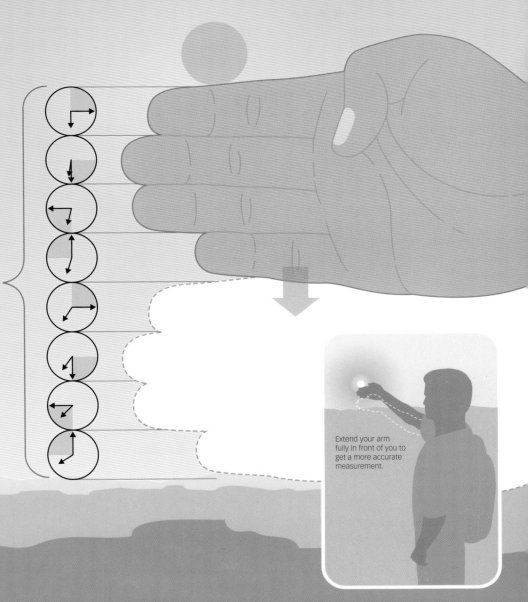

Straighten your arm away from your body, and hold your hand just below the sun (don't look right at the sun!). Now count the fingers between the sun and the horizon. Each finger counts for about fifteen minutes (so each hand represents one hour). The closer you are to the Earth's poles, the less accurate this trick will be.

Extend your arm fully in front of you to get a more accurate measurement.

First, locate the Big Dipper (also known as the Plough). Imagine a line between the two stars at the end of the Big Dipper's bowl. Extend that line five times, and you'll hit Polaris, the North Star (it's also the end of the Little Dipper's handle).

ursa major

polaris
(north star)

ursa minor
(little dipper)

big dipper
(plough)

When you're in the Northern Hemisphere, finding the North Star is the handiest way to orient yourself at night.

The dark patches you see on the moon are ancient basins filled with hardened lava, or basalt It's easy for us to see shapes in these basins, leading to the moon myths and stories many cultures have told for thousands of years.

Take a close look.
What do you see?

man in the moon
Europe and
the Americas

rabbit
China, Japan, Korea,
Mesoamerica

person carrying sticks
England, Australia,
Germany, Ancient Egypt

crab
South Pacific

frog
Peru, Angola, China

The moon doesn't rotate as it circles the Earth, and the same part of the moon is always facing the sun. But we see different moon phases because we see the moon's bright face from a different angle each night.

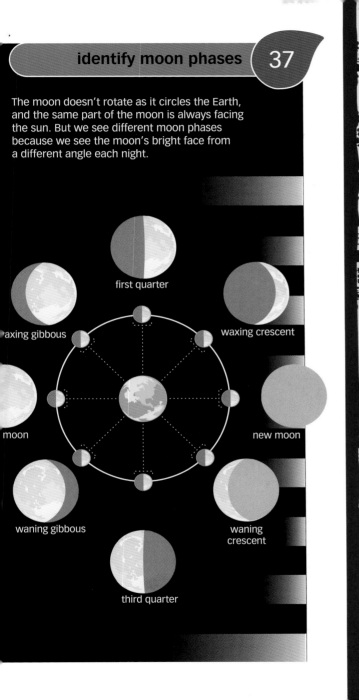

first quarter

waxing crescent

waxing gibbous

new moon

moon

waning gibbous

waning crescent

third quarter

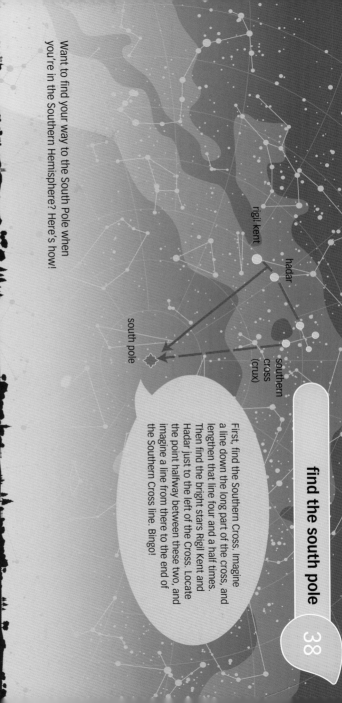

Want to find your way to the South Pole when you're in the Southern Hemisphere? Here's how!

rigil kent

hadar

south pole

southern cross (crux)

First, find the Southern Cross. Imagine a line down the long part of the cross, and lengthen that line four and a half times. Then find the bright stars Rigil Kent and Hadar just to the left of the Cross. Locate the point halfway between these two, and imagine a line from there to the end of the Southern Cross line. Bingo!

find the south pole 38

39 pitch a tent on the beach

Use damp sand to scrub dishes.

Camp well above the line of debris marking high tide.

Don't bring glass bottles.

A tarp lean-to provides shade.

Keep towels and a brush handy at the tent's opening.

Weight tent lines and bury in sand instead of using spikes.

Fully extinguish fires before burying coals.

40 set up a snow camp

Pack down a flat spot with skis, then pitch tent on top.

Don't use camp stove inside tent.

Don't pitch tent in avalanche-prone areas.

Tie tent lines to rocks and bury in the snow.

Dig a pit at tent opening for putting on and removing boots.

Run melted snow through a coffee filter before drinking.

Don't feed the wildlife!

Camp well away from pesky insect nests.

Hold a flame to leeches to remove; don't pull.

Leave perfume and deodorant at home.

Sleep on a raised platform with a rain tarp and mosquito netting.

Shake out sleeping bags before getting in.

Pitch tent at least 25 ft (7.5 m) above any water source.

Seal food in plastic containers and store outside of tent.

Camp on high ground, but avoid dangerous exposed ridges or peaks.

Keep your distance from wildlife.

Store extra drinks in the shade.

Pitch tent facing away from the east to avoid a sunrise awakening.

Bring (and drink!) 1 gal (3.75 l) of water per person per day.

Shake out your shoes before putting them on!

Secure tent lines to rebar, then top with plastic bottles to protect feet and ankles!

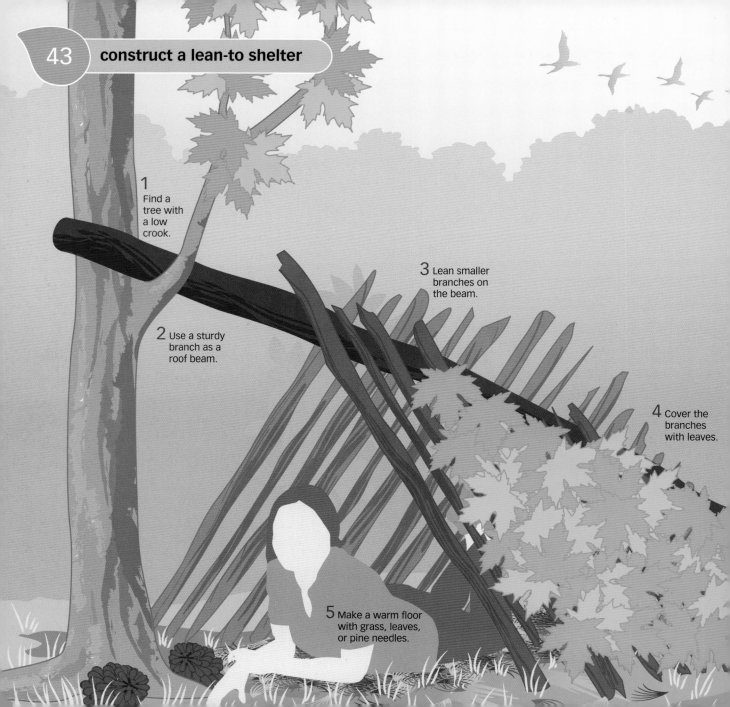

construct a lean-to shelter

1 Find a tree with a low crook.

2 Use a sturdy branch as a roof beam.

3 Lean smaller branches on the beam.

4 Cover the branches with leaves.

5 Make a warm floor with grass, leaves, or pine needles.

If you'd like to drink your found water, be sure to boil it first—it can be full of gross stuff, like bacteria.

Tie a towel below your knee.

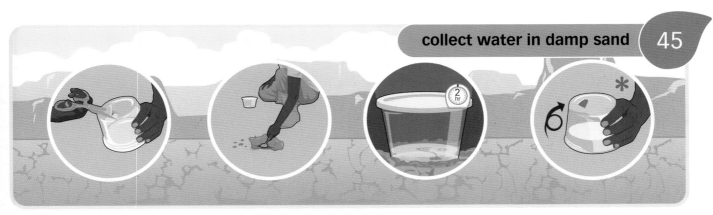

7 mi (11 km)

6 mi (10 km)

4 mi (6 km)

cirrus

cirrocumulus

cirrostratus

altocumulus

cumulonimbus

predict a rainstorm

Many cultures believe that nature gives clues right before a rain. Watch for these signs from around the world, and you may never get caught in a surprise shower again!

2 mi (3 km)

0 m (0 km)

cumulus

contrail

stratus

stratocumulus

nimbostratus

The weather vane spins around twice.

Spiders leave their webs.

Cats wash behind their ears.

Doors and windows are hard to open.

Crows fly low to the ground.

Ants move their eggs to higher ground.

Tree leaves flip over.

Grass is dry in the morning.

Cows lie down.

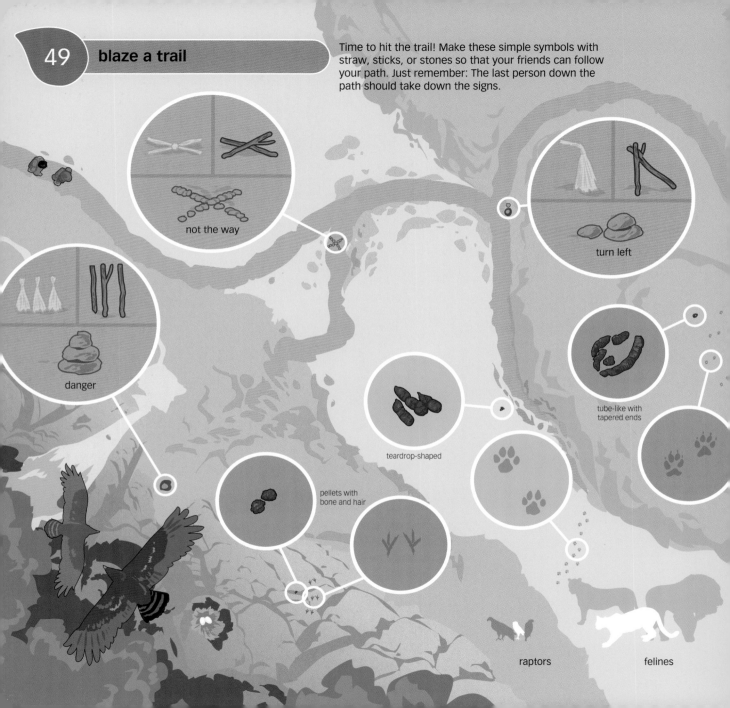

blaze a trail

Time to hit the trail! Make these simple symbols with straw, sticks, or stones so that your friends can follow your path. Just remember: The last person down the path should take down the signs.

not the way

turn left

danger

tube-like with tapered ends

teardrop-shaped

pellets with bone and hair

raptors

felines

turn right

head this way

When you're out trekking, look for animal prints and scat. Then use this guide to figure out what critters have been in your neck of the woods.

oval with a pointed end

small, circular pellets

looks like pencil lead

canines

deer family

rabbit family

rodents

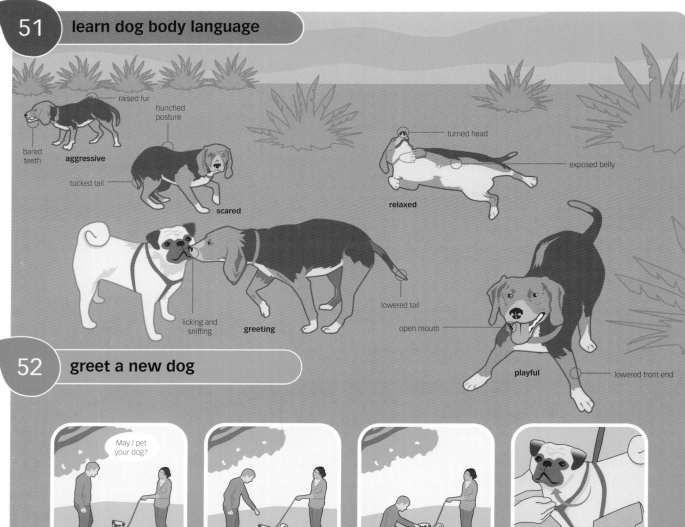

raised fur

hunched posture

bared teeth **aggressive**

tucked tail

scared

turned head

exposed belly

relaxed

licking and sniffing **greeting**

lowered tail

open mouth

playful

lowered front end

52 **greet a new dog**

May I pet your dog?

Check with the owner first.

Approach slowly from the front.

Let the dog sniff your fist.

Pet your new friend under the chin first.

raised tail

forward ears

flattened ears

alert

annoyed

twitching tail

exposed belly

narrowed
pupils

swishing tail

happy

bristled fur

blinking eyes

attacking

scared

crouching

Put some baby food
on your fingers.

Gently dab it
on his nose.

Let him get
a good taste.

Once he's won
over, pet him.

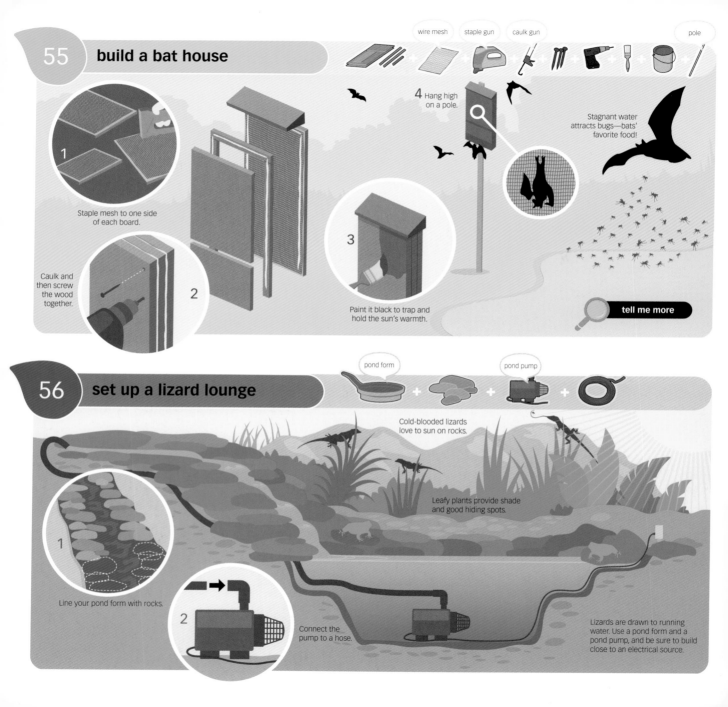

55 build a bat house

wire mesh | staple gun | caulk gun | pole

1 Staple mesh to one side of each board.

2 Caulk and then screw the wood together.

3 Paint it black to trap and hold the sun's warmth.

4 Hang high on a pole.

Stagnant water attracts bugs—bats' favorite food!

tell me more

56 set up a lizard lounge

pond form | pond pump

Cold-blooded lizards love to sun on rocks.

Leafy plants provide shade and good hiding spots.

1 Line your pond form with rocks.

2 Connect the pump to a hose.

Lizards are drawn to running water. Use a pond form and a pond pump, and be sure to build close to an electrical source.

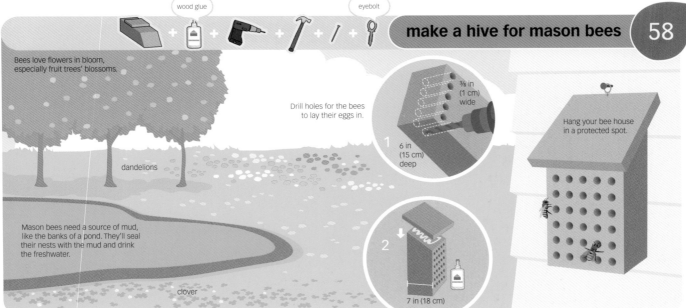

hanging tray

silk flowers

Get colorful! You'll attract more butterflies with a rainbow of flowers.

To attract male butterflies, fill a bowl with sand, then add water, salt, and a little fruit juice.

Dig a hole and bury the bowl up to the rim.

Decorate.

1

Hang no higher than the yard's tallest flowers.

2

Add pieces of rotting fruit.

wood glue

eyebolt

Bees love flowers in bloom, especially fruit trees' blossoms.

Drill holes for the bees to lay their eggs in.

⅜ in (1 cm) wide

1   6 in (15 cm) deep

dandelions

Mason bees need a source of mud, like the banks of a pond. They'll seal their nests with the mud and drink the freshwater.

clover

2

7 in (18 cm)

Hang your bee house in a protected spot.

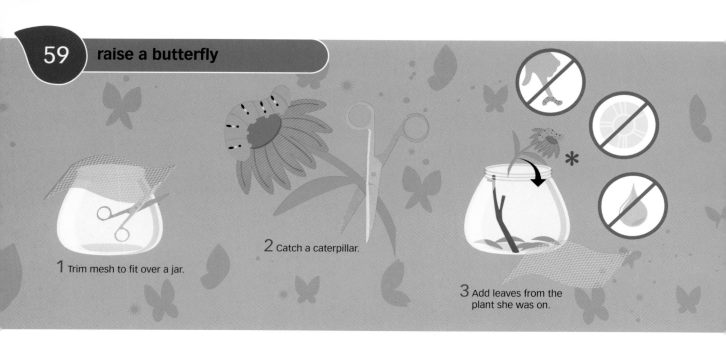

59 raise a butterfly

1 Trim mesh to fit over a jar.

2 Catch a caterpillar.

3 Add leaves from the plant she was on.

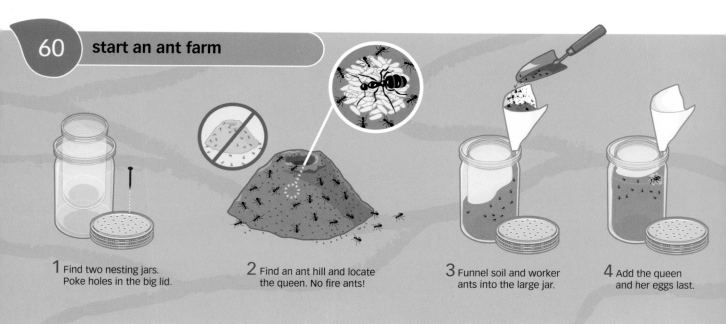

60 start an ant farm

1 Find two nesting jars. Poke holes in the big lid.

2 Find an ant hill and locate the queen. No fire ants!

3 Funnel soil and worker ants into the large jar.

4 Add the queen and her eggs last.

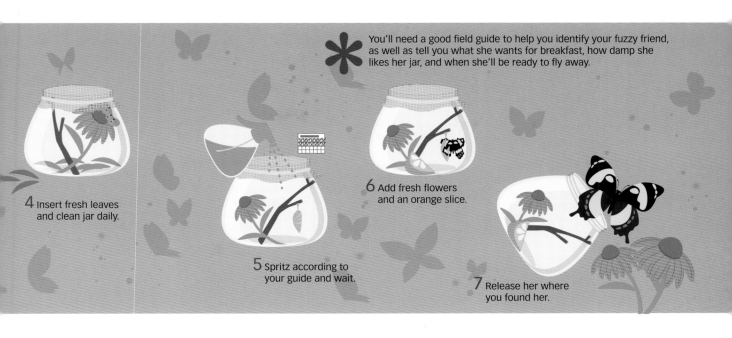

You'll need a good field guide to help you identify your fuzzy friend, as well as tell you what she wants for breakfast, how damp she likes her jar, and when she'll be ready to fly away.

4 Insert fresh leaves and clean jar daily.

5 Spritz according to your guide and wait.

6 Add fresh flowers and an orange slice.

7 Release her where you found her.

5 Soak a cotton ball in water, and bread crumbs in honey.

6 Feed your new pets every ten days.

7 Cover. The ants will think they're underground and make their tunnels.

8 Lift the paper to check out the ant-farm action, then re-cover.

predict bunny friendships

What's better than one bunny? Two! But be aware that not all bunny matches end in friendship—some pairs will struggle for territory, while others will be indifferent to one another. Use this as your guide to rabbit compatibility.

two males
possible aggression

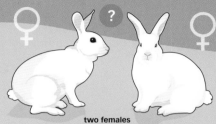

two females
may take a while to
warm up to each other

male and female
love at first sight

two babies
instant friends

baby and unrelated adult
may not bond

introduce two rabbits

Introduce in a neutral
spot.

Give them time to
hang out.

Stop aggression with
water.

Hope for love.

Many animals behave strangely before a disaster like a tsunami or an earthquake. Take care if your pet is acting oddly, or if you see any of these behaviors.

Hoofed animals may huddle together in open areas.

Farm animals may pace or refuse to be tied or led into their barns.

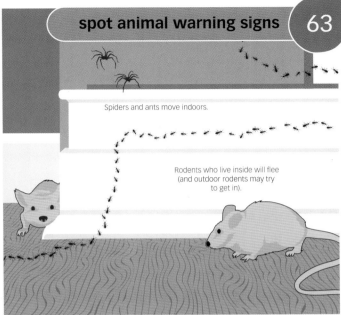

Spiders and ants move indoors.

Rodents who live inside will flee (and outdoor rodents may try to get in).

Confined animals, like those in the zoo, may try to escape.

Hibernating animals will wake early and leave their dens.

Birds will push eggs from their nests.

spy on sea life

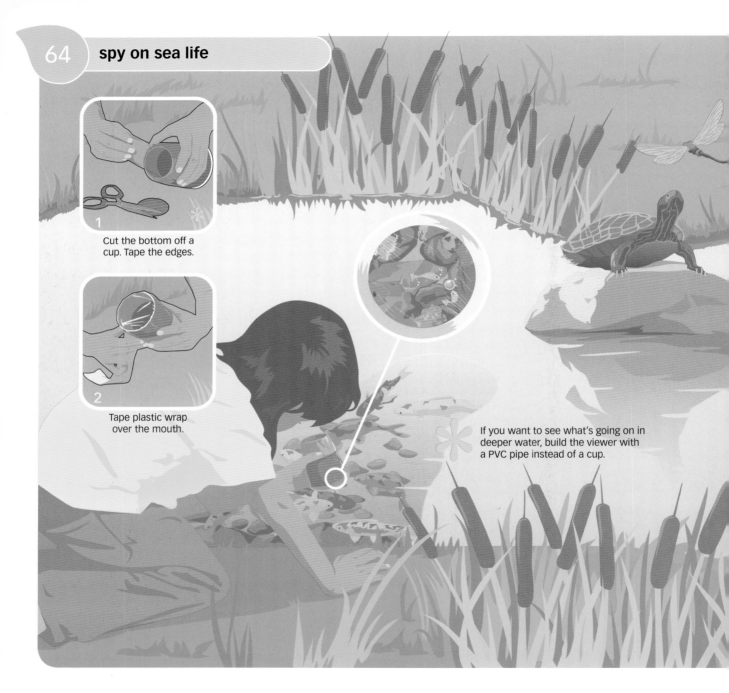

1

Cut the bottom off a cup. Tape the edges.

2

Tape plastic wrap over the mouth.

If you want to see what's going on in deeper water, build the viewer with a PVC pipe instead of a cup.

Lay smaller sticks across the long sticks.

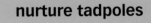

Layer with mud and smaller sticks until the flow of water stops.

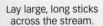

* Don't leave it to beavers to take the dam apart. Dismantle it yourself when you're done playing!

Lay large, long sticks across the stream.

nurture tadpoles 66

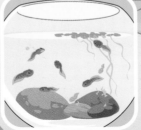

Collect tadpoles and pond water.

Place in shade and leave still.

3 months

Add frozen lettuce or fish food twice a day.

Release the frogs into the same pond.

tell me more

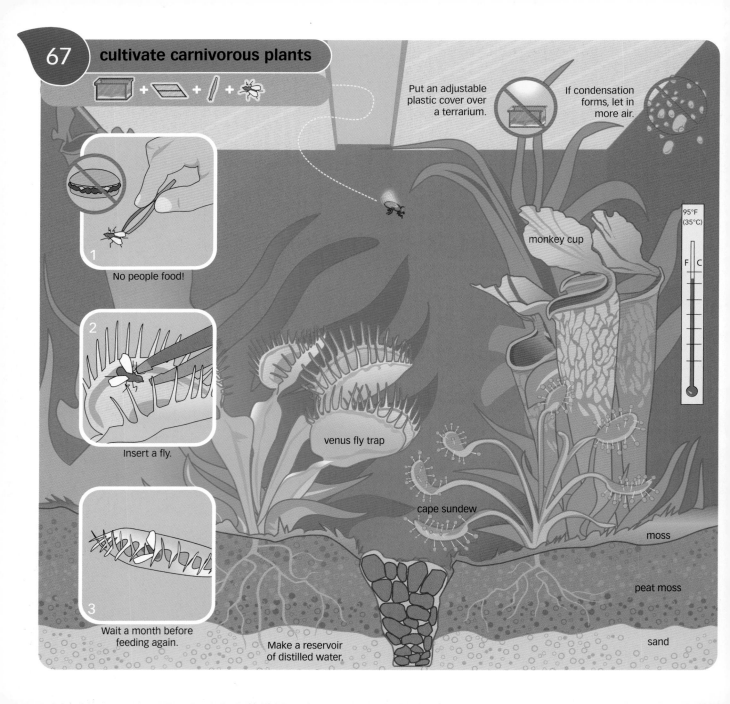

cultivate carnivorous plants

Put an adjustable plastic cover over a terrarium.

If condensation forms, let in more air.

No people food!

1

Insert a fly.

2

Wait a month before feeding again.

3

monkey cup

95°F (35°C)

F C

venus fly trap

cape sundew

moss

peat moss

Make a reservoir of distilled water.

sand

hollow out a birdhouse 68

 + + + +

wood glue   clothesline

1. Give your gourd a good scrubbing.

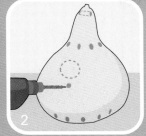

2. Drill holes. Cut a high entrance.

3. Scoop out the insides.

4. Glue in a perch.

5. Thread a piece of clothesline.

6. Hang in early spring.

personalize a melon 69

 + +

1. Plant the melon seeds.

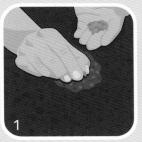

2. Water.

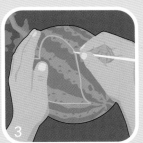

3. Etch shallow lines with a wood skewer.

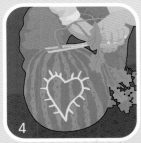

4. The melon will heal, revealing your art!

+ + + + +

1

Pluck some pretty
flowers, stem and all.

2

Slice thicker
flowers in half.

✳ If you want to preserve your bouquets but keep
them looking full, hang them upside down to dry.

3

Set on newspaper
in a heavy book.

4

Fold the newspaper.

5

Close the book and
add a weight.

6

Arrange on acid-free
paper and frame.

acid-free
paper

enamel pot vinegar

2 c (500 g)
ground coffee beans

3 c (750 g) blueberries

4 c (1 kg) spinach

4 c (1 kg) beets or cranberries

*
4 c (1 kg)
chopped cabbage

Coarsely chop
red cabbage.

15 min

1 q (1 l) water
2 tbsp vinegar

Simmer.

Strain out the cabbage.

15 min

Add the garment. Simmer
longer for darker coloring.

18 hr

Refrigerate overnight.

Hang outside to dry.

* Your kitchen is full of natural fabric
dyes. Substitute these ingredients
for the cabbage in this recipe to get
a rainbow of tasty earth tones!

3 c (750 g) loose tea

72 save poppy seeds

73 sprout an avocado pit

74 dry tomato seeds

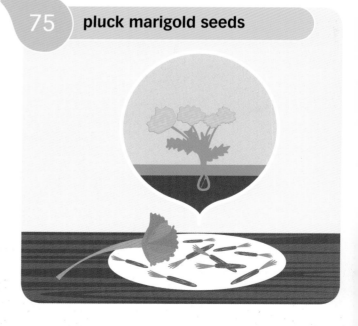

75 pluck marigold seeds

+ + + wire mesh + + +

Shred paper.

Fill a blender with equal parts paper and water.

Blend at low speed until you have mush.

Carefully stir in seeds.

Roll the pulp onto a screen.

Turn on a fan to make the paper dry more quickly.

Gently peel off the dry paper.

Send a plantable greeting card!

sow a seed bomb

  + compost + red clay

½ c (70 g) seeds

¾ c (200 g) compost

1

Combine seeds and compost.

1⅓ c (350 g) red clay

2

Mix with clay.

While strolling with a parent, keep an eye out for spots in your neighborhood that could be greener and prettier. Target these places with your seed bombs for guerilla-style beautification!

1 c (240 ml) water

3

Add water and mix.

4

Roll marble-size "bombs."

5

Dry in the sun.

6

Launch before a rain.

Pick a hardy plant that won't require much care, and that is indigenous to your area.

 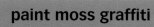

Crumble the moss;
pour in water.

handful of moss

2 c (500 ml)
water

Add sugar and buttermilk.

½ tsp
sugar

2 c (475 ml)
buttermilk

Pulse blender until
gel forms.

Paint onto wood or
rough concrete.

Mist weekly.

Watch your art grow.

compost in your backyard

Use a backyard compost pile to keep your organic waste out of a landfill and provide your garden plants with superfood. Layer waste as shown, water, and turn it with a shovel. You'll know it has transformed into sweet, nutritious compost when you can't discern any bits in it—when it's just dark, rich dirt.

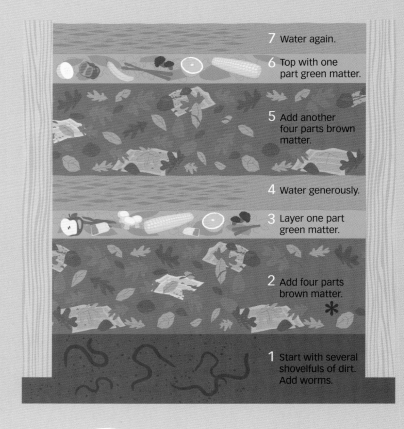

7 Water again.

6 Top with one part green matter.

5 Add another four parts brown matter.

4 Water generously.

3 Layer one part green matter.

2 Add four parts brown matter. ✳

1 Start with several shovelfuls of dirt. Add worms.

These items attract vermin. Compost them at your own risk.

Water the pile weekly.

Turn with a shovel as needed.

 The ideal brown matter is carbon-rich: mostly dead leaves, with some newspaper, wood, and sawdust added. Green matter is nitrogen-rich, composed of items like veggies, eggs, green plant leaves, and tea. Tasty!

A patch of dirt and a plan is all you need to grow your very own bounty of vegetables!

Divide plot into 12-in-by-12-in (30-cm-by-30-cm) squares.

Choose vegetables that grow tall to increase how many plants you harvest.

Plant tall plants at plot's edge to keep their shadows off nearby plants.

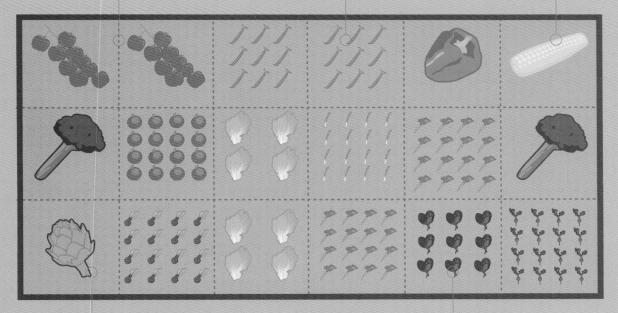

Variety is the spice of life! Plant and enjoy a wide range of nutritious crops year-round.

Put shallow-rooted plants next to deep-rooted ones so they don't compete for water.

Replant as soon as you harvest.

Fertilize soil year-round.

dig up a lost civilization

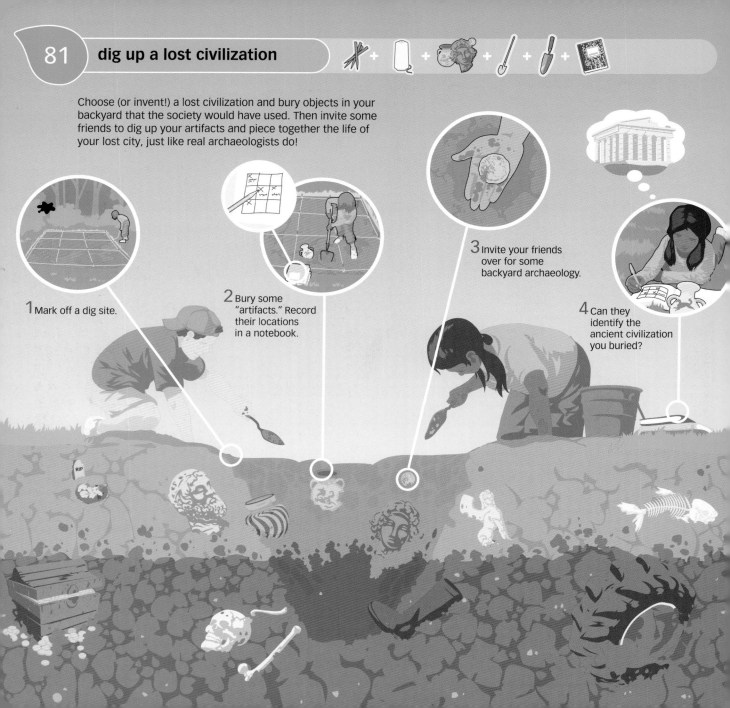

Choose (or invent!) a lost civilization and bury objects in your backyard that the society would have used. Then invite some friends to dig up your artifacts and piece together the life of your lost city, just like real archaeologists do!

1 Mark off a dig site.

2 Bury some "artifacts." Record their locations in a notebook.

3 Invite your friends over for some backyard archaeology.

4 Can they identify the ancient civilization you buried?

1. Pick an area with lots of foot traffic.

2. Prepare the plaster as the package instructs.

3. Carefully fill a footprint.

4. Let the plaster set, then remove.

5. Brush off your fossil.

6. Try to figure out who made it!

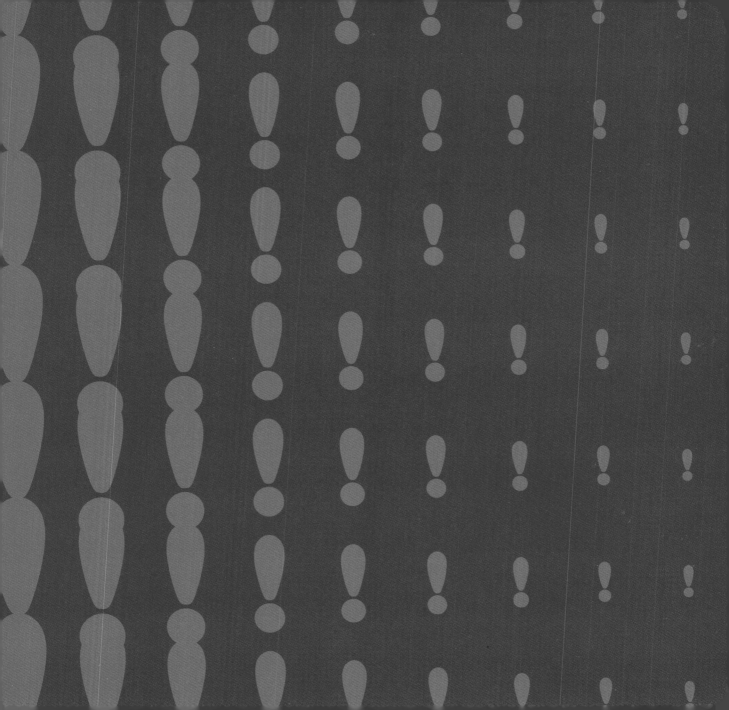

tell me more

Pssst! Want to know more about a project in this book? This handy section is full of trivia, history, and extra expert advice that will help you tackle certain activities or better understand what's so awesome about them.

7 tell time with a potato

The acid in a potato is conductive, meaning electrically charged atoms can move around easily inside it. As the potato's acid eats away at the nail's zinc, a chemical reaction attracts electrons from the copper wire. The easiest way for these copper electrons to get to the nail is through the wires you've clamped on. The flow of these electrons is the electricity that powers the clock.

3 bend water with static

Everything in the world is made of atoms, and atoms are made of positive, negative, and neutral electric charges. These are known as protons (positive), electrons (negative), and neutrons (neutral). When certain objects, like your hair and a comb, come in contact, the electrons jump from one to the other. This leads to a buildup of negative charges on one object—in this case, on the comb.

Because opposites attract, these electrons will be drawn to positive charges (a state called static electricity). That's why the electrons on the negatively charged comb can tug other positively charged objects (like the torn tissue or stream of water) toward the comb. This attraction is also why the electrons on the television screen can jump to the tinfoil and why the electrons move from the balloon to the lightbulb: these negative charges want to take over positively charged areas! And when they do, the static electricity they generate can set off sparks or even make a little music.

Want to try one more static trick? Use static to separate salt and pepper! Make a small pile of salt and pepper on a flat surface. Rub a balloon vigorously against a wool sweater, then slowly bring the balloon near the salt and pepper pile—the pepper will fly up and stick to the balloon, leaving the salt.

13 send secrets by morse code

In the days before phones and radio, it could take people months to send a message across a long distance. In 1844, Samuel Morse popularized the telegraph, a device for sending electric signals across miles of cable. Messages were written in Morse code, a system of dots and dashes that symbolize letters and punctuation. It was very handy during World Wars I and II.

16 turn the world upside down

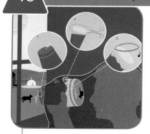

This device is also known as a camera obscura. Why does the image flip upside down, exactly? As light passes through the tiny hole, the light that is coming up from the bottom of the scene continues going up and the light shining down from the top of the scene continues traveling down. These separate light waves hit the paper screen, and the top and bottom are reversed.

Sun prints are also known as cyanotypes (cyan is a deep shade of blue). The paper is coated in a chemical that turns blue after exposure to sunlight. By placing objects over parts of the paper, you block the sunlight from reaching the surface beneath them, so those parts don't turn blue. When you wash the chemicals off with water, the parts of the chemical that didn't turn blue are washed away, and the paper gets bluer as it dries. Cyanotypes, invented in 1842, were popular with engineers and architects, who needed to reproduce notes and plans in the days before copy machines. They called their cyanotypes "blueprints."

You can make beautiful sun prints by cutting shapes out of thick paper and arranging them into scenes.

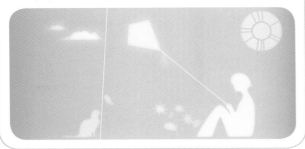

Bats, when they're not living in caves, prefer to sleep and raise young in trees—ideally in a space where bark has split off from a tree trunk. Deforestation means many bats have nowhere to live, so the best thing you can do for them is to offer a warm, secluded spot that mimics these tree homes. Your bat house should be tall and narrow, with a tiny entrance slot at the bottom and a scratchy interior surface that the bats can climb up and cling to.

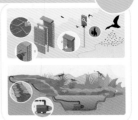

So why go to all this trouble for these little critters? A bat eats hundreds, sometimes thousands, of bugs per hour, keeping your backyard free from pests that munch on your plants. Plus, bats are pollinators, which means they spread pollen between plants, causing new plants to grow that other creatures can then eat. So these dark-winged critters play a crucial part in our ecosystem: when bat populations decline, other local creatures will suffer as well.

While premade bat houses are available at garden stores and online, making them isn't hard. Our instructions are a good start; you can also check with a local conservation group to find out what cribs will be popular with your local bats.

Your leaf-and-needle compass works on a familiar premise: that opposites attract. The Earth's poles are magnetized, so the magnetized needle is attracted to them and aligns itself with the north-south axis. It's important that there are no other magnetized items near the leaf—they can interfere with your compass's reading. It also helps to keep the leaf out of the wind.

When raising your tadpoles, don't overcrowd your tank. Each tadpole needs a gallon (3¾ l) of water. After a few weeks, the tadpoles will stop eating the food you give them, and their tails will start to disappear. Don't freak out! This means they are growing fine. As soon as little legs appear, place some large rocks in the tank so the tadpoles can climb out of the water to breathe.

index

about the authors

Sarah Hines Stephens first learned to cook in order to get out of doing the dishes, and she still prefers making messes to cleaning them. One of three creative sisters, Sarah hails from generations of do-it-yourselfers: quilters, artists, writers, and gardeners. When Sarah is not facilitating semiexplosive science experiments and kid-friendly crafts, she writes books for kids. She has written more than sixty books. She lives with her husband and two children in a home filled with glitter, fabric scraps, glue, and power tools.

Bethany Mann is Sarah's sister and partner in creative mess-making. With a rallying cry of, "Hey, we could totally make that ourselves!" she has fearlessly led her family and friends in numerous craft adventures. These days Bethany channels her artistic powers for good by using recycled materials and growing vegetables. Her projects have been featured in craft books for adults and on DIY TV. She lives with her husband, teenage son, and a menagerie of rescued pets in the mountains near Santa Cruz, California. Read her blog at www.bitterbettyindustries.blogspot.com.

WELDON OWEN INC.

CEO, President Terry Newell

VP, Sales and New Business Development Amy Kaneko

VP, Publisher Roger Shaw

Creative Director Kelly Booth

Executive Editor Mariah Bear

Senior Editor Lucie Parker

Project Editor Frances Reade

Assistant Editors Emelie Griffin, Katharine Moore

Senior Designers Stephanie Tang, Meghan Hildebrand

Designer Delbarr Moradi

Illustration Coordinators Sheila Masson, Conor Buckley

Production Director Chris Hemesath

Production Manager Michelle Duggan

weldon**owen**

415 Jackson Street, Suite 200
San Francisco, CA 94111
Telephone: 415 291 0100
Fax: 415 291 8841
www.weldonowen.com

A division of

BONNIER

Do It Now! Science: Wild Experiments & Outdoor Adventures

Excerpted from *Show Off,* first published by Candlewick Press in 2009.

Library of Congress Control Number: 2012932624

ISBN 13: 978-1-61628-392-6

ISBN 10: 1-61628-392-0

10 9 8 7 6 5 4 3 2 1
2016   2015   2014   2013   2012

Printed in China by 1010 Printing International Ltd

Typeset in Vectora LH

SHOW ME NOW™

A Show Me Now Book.
Show Me Now is a trademark of Weldon Owen Inc.

Special thanks to:

Storyboarders

Esy Casey, Julumarie Joy Cornista, Sarah Lynn Duncan, Chris Hall, Paula Rogers, Jamie Spinello, Brandi Valenza

Illustration specialists

Hayden Foell, Raymond Larrett, Ross Sublett

Editorial and research support team

Ian Cannon, Marc Caswell, Mollie Church, Elizabeth Dougherty, Kat Engh, Alex Eros, Justin Goers, Sarah Gurman, Susan Jonaitis, Peter Masiak, Grace Newell, Jennifer Newens, Paul Ozzello, Ben Rosenberg, Hiya Swanhuyser

Kid-reviewer panel

Emma Arlen, Leah Cohen, Sally Elton, Whitman Hall, Tesserae Honor, Nami Kaneko, Emily Newell, Eloise Shaw, Georgia Shaw

Illustration credits

Front cover
Britt Hanson: avocado pit **Liberum Donum (Juan Calle, Santiago Calle, Andres Penagos):** potato clock **Vincent Perea:** carnivorous plants **Gabhor Utomo:** volcano

Back cover
Britt Hanson: butterfly jar, lava lamp **Joshua Kemble:** dye pot, robot **Raymond Larrett:** initial crystal **Liberum Donum (Juan Calle, Santiago Calle, Andres Penagos):** digging, fossilized footprints, glowing shadow **Vincent Perea:** cat **Gabhor Utomo:** bag on tree branch, fake fingerprint, invisible ink, magnet, orange-carton periscope, tadpoles **Tina Cash Walsh:** dried flowers, seed paper

Interiors
Key: bg = background; bd = border; fr = frames; ex = extra art

Esy Casey: 19 bg **Liberum Donum (Juan Calle, Santiago Calle, Andres Penagos):** 1, 7, 22, 30, 42 fr, 49–50, 66 fr, 81, 82 fr **Hayden Foell:** 31, 60, 80 **Britt Hanson:** 3–6, 13, 16, 23, 42 bg, 59, 72–75 **Gary Henricks:** 27 **Joshua Kemble:** 25, 71 **Vic Kulihin:** 24, 28 **Raymond Larrett:** 8–9, 21, 63 **Vincent Perea:** 17, 51, 53–54, 67 **Paula Rogers:** 61–62 **Ross Sublett:** 57 fr **Bryon Thompson:** 2, 34, 43, 55–58 **Wil Tirion:** 35, 38 **Taylor Tucek:** 19–20 **Gabhor Utomo:** 10–12, 14–15, 18, 26, 33, 36–37, 44–48, 64–65, 66 bg **Tina Cash Walsh:** 52, 68–70, 76–78, 82 bg **Mary Zins:** 32